THE OFFICIAL
EVERTON FC
ANNUAL 2021

Written by **Darren Griffiths**
Designed by **Jodie Clark**

A Grange Publication

ISBN 978-1-913034-95-5

GRAEME
SHARP
1980 – 1991
Appearances – 425 (21)
Goals – 159

CONTENTS

CARLO
ANCELOTTI

> I love the passion Evertonians have for their team and the connection we have with our supporters is a big strength for us.

This is a great club with a rich history and a very passionate fanbase. The name of Everton carries a significant weight across the continent, so when I learned of the opportunity to manage this club I immediately wanted to know more.

There is a clear vision from the owner and the board to deliver trophies and that is something that appeals to me as a manager. I am thrilled at the prospect of being able to work with everybody at the club to help make that vision a reality. The way I was welcomed before my first game against Burnley was a special moment for me. It was like no other reception that I've had. We feel a responsibility to repay that support and every decision we make is with a view to Everton competing with the top clubs in this country and across Europe.

You Evertonians have an enormous part to play in what we are trying to achieve. I know how much you love our creative players and strikers, but I also see and hear the appreciation you have when the players make a big effort. It is fantastic when I listen to the cheering after a strong tackle or when a player sprints to close down his opponent.

I brought Chelsea to Goodison when we were top of the Premier League but guys like John Terry, Frank Lampard and Ashley Cole said to expect one of our toughest nights of the season. They were right! It felt like playing against one big family joining together.

I love the passion Evertonians have for their team and the connection we have with our supporters is a big strength for us.

I want to say thank you for your backing and how you have supported me from the moment I joined the club. I have been fortunate to manage some great teams around the world and I can honestly say that Evertonians are special.

I look forward to what we can achieve together in the future ...

25 FACTS ABOUT ...
CARLO ANCELOTTI

Carlo started his professional playing career with Parma in the third tier of Italian football in the 1976/77 season.

In 1979 he joined Roma in Serie A.

With Roma, Carlo won the Serie A League title in 1982-83 and won the Italian Cup four times.

In 1987, he signed for AC Milan, where he was very successful.

Whilst in Milan, Carlo won two more Serie A League titles and two European Cups.

He made his debut for the Italian national team in 1981 against Holland – and scored in a 1-1 draw.

It was a great start, but it was to be the only goal he would ever score for Italy!

In total, Carlo won 26 caps for Italy and played against England in the 3rd/4th place play-off in the 1990 World Cup.

His first coaching job was with the Italian national team.

He was the assistant manager when Italy reached the 1994 World Cup final, only to lose on penalties to Brazil.

Carlo's first manager's job was with Reggiana in Serie B and he led them to promotion in 1996.

In 1999 he became the manager of Juventus and won the Intertoto Cup in his first season.

From Juve, Carlo returned to AC Milan as their new manager in 2001.

Back at Milan, where he had enjoyed so much success as a player, he won another Serie A title, the Italian Cup and two Champions League finals.

The second of those Champions League wins was against Liverpool in 2007 – gaining revenge for the loss in Istanbul two years earlier.

Carlo in action for Roma

Taking on Diego Maradona during his AC Milan days

Playing against England in the 1990 World Cup

In 2009, Carlo came to England to manage Chelsea.

In 2010 he led them to the double of Premier League and FA Cup.

His last game as Chelsea manager was a 1-0 defeat against Everton at Goodison when Jermaine Beckford scored a wonder-goal!

Carlo's next club was Paris St. Germain, where he won the French Ligue 1 title in 2013.

He then left France to succeed Jose Mourinho as the manager of Real Madrid.

In his first season at Madrid he won the Copa del Rey (Spanish FA Cup) and the Champions League.

In 2016, Carlo replaced Pep Guardiola as the manager of Bayern Munich.

He won the German Bundesliga title in his first season.

Carlo returned to Italy for the 2018/19 season when he took over at Napoli.

In December 2019 he came back to the Premier League to become the manager of Everton.

Arriving at Goodison Park!

Winning the Champions League as AC Milan manager

Champions League winner with Real Madrid

Premier League winner with Chelsea

ALLAN

LEARN ALL ABOUT ME ...!

My full name is
Allan Marques Loureiro.

I was born in
Rio de Janeiro, in Brazil.

My birthday is 8 January 1991.

I started my
playing career
with an amateur
team in Rio de
Janeiro called
Madureira.

My first professional
club was Vasco de
Gama, who I joined
in 2009.

In 2011 I was part of the
Brazil team that won
the FIFA Under-20
World Cup. Oscar, Phillipe
Coutinho, Danilo and
Gabriel were among my
team-mates. We beat
Portugal in the final.

In 2012 I came to Europe to sign for Italian side Udinese.

At the end of my first season we finished 5th in Serie A to qualify for the Europa League.

After three seasons with Udinese I moved to Napoli.

My first manager at Napoli was Maurizio Sarri, who later managed Chelsea in the Premier League.

Among my team-mates were Jorginho and Gonzalo Higuain, who would also both join Chelsea!

On the ball for Napoli

In 2017, Napoli finished 3rd in Serie A to qualify for the Champions League and the season after we finished 2nd in the table.

For the 2018/19 season, Sarri was replaced as the manager of Napoli by Carlo Ancelotti and we defeated Liverpool 1-0 in the Champions League group stage.

Sadly, we didn't make it from the group and we dropped into the Europa League where we lost in the quarter-final to an Arsenal team that included Alex Iwobi.

In 2018 I made my full international debut for Brazil.

In 2019 I was part of the Brazil squad, along with Richarlison, that won the Copa America. I came on as a substitute in the final, replacing Everton! (Everton Soares plays for Benfica).

In 2020 I was in the Napoli team that won the Coppa Italia, beating Juventus in the final.

In September 2020 I signed for Everton!

Copa America action for Brazil in 2019

THINK YOU KNOW ALL THERE IS TO KNOW ABOUT GOODISON PARK ...?

THINK AGAIN!

Goodison Park was built in 1892.

The original site of the stadium was called Mere Green Field

The very first turnstiles at Goodison Park cost £7 each!

Goodison was the first purpose-built stadium for football in the country.

The first game at the stadium was on 2nd September 1892 and Everton defeated Bolton Wanderers 4-2.

That was an exhibition game – and the first League fixture was played the very next day when Everton drew 2-2 with Nottingham Forest. It was Forest's first ever league match.

The 1894 FA Cup final was played at Goodison – and so was the 1910 final replay.

The stadium grew and grew and in 1931, Everton was the first club to install dug-outs at the side of the pitch.

In 1928, the legendary Dixie Dean created a record at Goodison that may never be beaten when he scored his 60th league goal in a single season. Dean died at Goodison in 1980.

Dixie Dean broke a goalscoring record at Goodison – and he has a statue at the stadium

Goodison suffered bomb damage in 1940

In 1940, Goodison suffered bomb damage during the Second World War. The Gwladys Street end was hit by a German explosive and the cost of repair was £5,000.

An early game at Goodison

Goodison in the 1960s

Goodison Now

The record attendance is 78,299 for a game against Liverpool in September 1948. That figure will never be surpassed.

In 1957 floodlights were added.

The first under-soil heating system in English football was installed in 1958.

Goodison Park was one of the grounds chosen to host matches during the 1966 World Cup.

Brazil and the great Pele played their group games at the stadium.

Goodison was also the venue for the 1966 World Cup semi-final between West Germany and Russia.

Pele in World Cup action at Goodison in 1966, with the church in the background

The church

It is the only stadium in England that is attached to a church. Where the Main Stand and the Gwladys Street meet, is the church of St Luke the Evangelist.

The lowest ever attendance came in December 1988 when just 3,703 fans watched a Simod Cup game against Millwall.

In 2016, the stands behind each goal were renamed – The Howard Kendall Gwladys Street Stand and the Sir Philip Carter Park Stand.

Goodison Park has staged more top-division games than any other stadium in the country.

MICHAEL KEANE

SIXTY GRAND, SIXTY GRAND ...

SEAMUS COLEMAN!

YOU KNOW HOW THE SONG GOES!

Everton's hugely popular skipper came to the club from Sligo Rovers in 2009 for the princely price of sixty thousand pounds. Seamus Coleman is probably the best 'value for money' signing that Everton have ever made!

But even after all this time, and more than 300 appearances, he still sets himself the very highest of standards every day and he never allows himself to forget the first two years when he was trying to prove himself good enough to play for the Blues ...

Let's go back to the very beginning when you first came to Everton. You were a completely unknown player and had a lot of hard work ahead of you ...

Everton took a chance on me without a trial and I was off the back of a few unsuccessful trials at other clubs. In the two years after I came here, I never once thought that I'd made it. You have to keep proving yourself and that's true to this day. I was a reserve team player in the reserve team dressing room and those first two years were on trying to make a career for myself at Everton.

> **I WAS IN AWE OF WORKING WITH THE LIKES OF STEVEN PIENAAR, LOUIS SAHA, PHIL NEVILLE, LEIGHTON BAINES, PHIL JAGIELKA**

I had no mates outside of football. I was a quiet lad. I'd train, come home, go for a sleep then get my food. I'd go on PlayStation for an hour or two and ring home. Then I'd start to prepare for the next training session. That was my life for two years. Along the way, I played with players who had a lot more ability than me, but they didn't have the same focus and hunger and desire to make it as a professional footballer.

I had a fear of failure. I didn't want to be back home after two years, jumping on a flight with my tail between my legs to go and play League of Ireland football.

It was obviously very challenging for you ... were you unhappy at first?

I wouldn't want to say that I was unhappy in those initial two years. I was happy to be driving into a Premier League football club every day. I was in awe of working with the likes of Steven Pienaar, Louis Saha, Phil Neville, Leighton Baines, Phil Jagielka ... the list goes on, proper men, proper professionals.

I was homesick – but that fear of failure, I was never going to let people say 'It was a big step for him, it was asking a lot for him to make it.'

And now you're the captain! Does that mean you have to shout at the other players sometimes?

If I have to tell someone to sharpen up, I will. But I want players to understand that I am doing things for the right reasons. In the short term they might think that I am on their cases, but I want them to reach their potential and realise that they have massive opportunities.

You have to look in the mirror every day and ask 'Did I do everything I could for the club, my team-mates and the fans?' You never want to let yourself or the team down.

Looking towards the future, we know you've done your coaching badges...

I make notes on certain training sessions and situations. We are playing for one of the best managers in history and it is a great opportunity to learn from him. He might say something to a player, or deal with a situation in a certain way and sub-consciously you are logging it.

I love watching football, different managers and different styles of play. I am interested in formations and shape and how teams build from the back.

You have to make sacrifices, don't you, when you're a footballer - you have to do the right things off the pitch...?

You need to make sure you are professional. You're being paid by the club and can't be sitting around eating packets of crisps and unhealthy dinners. When I first came to Everton, I was living by myself. My girlfriend, who is now my wife, was studying in Dublin. She would fly over at weekends, make dinners and put them in the freezer to keep me going for the week.

LEIGHTON BAINES WAS A BIG INFLUENCE ON COLEMAN

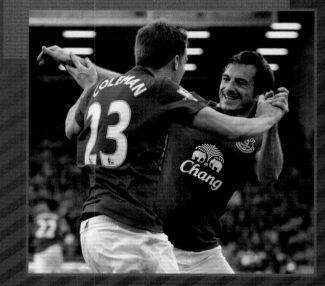

Sum up your attitude to being a footballer with Everton...

I want to impress every single day. If someone has a go at me in training because of giving the ball away, or a manager gives me a dressing down after a game because of my performance, it is no problem. But I would never want a manager or my team-mates to be able to say that I wasn't trying. That would be the biggest insult to me as a professional footballer. When I put my head on the pillow at night, I know I have given 100% and been a good team-mate.

I have had an unbelievable time at Everton, but I will keep saying, as loud as I can, unless I win a cup at this club, I will feel the job was never completed.

SEAMUS COLEMAN QUIZ

1 Who was the manager of Everton when I joined the club?

2 Which team did I join on loan from Everton ten years ago?

3 Who is my current international manager?

4 Who was the Everton captain before me?

5 Which other sport did I play before becoming a footballer?

ANSWERS ON PAGE 62

WHO AM I ...?

Here are twelve pictures of Everton players - playing for someone else! These were all taken early in their careers before they came to Goodison. All you need to do is name the player and the team he is playing for ...

1

PLAYER ....

CLUB ....

2

PLAYER ....

CLUB ....

3

PLAYER ....

CLUB ....

4

PLAYER ....

CLUB ....

5

PLAYER ....

CLUB ....

6

PLAYER ....

CLUB ....

7

PLAYER ....

CLUB ....

8

PLAYER ....

CLUB ....

9

PLAYER ....

CLUB ....

10

PLAYER ....

CLUB ....

11

PLAYER ....

CLUB ....

12

PLAYER ....

CLUB ....

Answers on pages 62-63

RICHARLISON

WHO AM I?

HERE'S AN EVERTON STAR WHO APPEARS TO BE TRYING TO CONTROL THE BALL WITH HIS FACE!

DO YOU KNOW WHO IT IS?

ANSWER

ANSWER ON PAGE 62

UNDER-18s

Paul Tait is the coach of the Everton Under-18s Academy team. He was a centre-forward in his playing days and was actually a youth team player himself with the Blues many years ago!

WHAT QUALITIES DO YOU LOOK FOR IN AN UNDER-18S PLAYER?

Well they've already shown a very good degree of ability to get to this level so we'll start to do a few sessions away from the football pitch, concentrating on behavioural qualities – such as never giving up, fighting for everything, showing a real desire to want to succeed. These are what all the top players have.

HOW IMPORTANT IS IT TO CONSTANTLY MONITOR MENTAL HEALTH AS WELL AS PHYSICAL HEALTH? YOU WERE AT EVERTON IN THE 1990S AND IT WASN'T A PRIORITY IN THOSE DAYS, WAS IT?

No it wasn't, it was just a case of 'get on with it' but thankfully things have changed and the emphasis on mental health is vitally important. I am certain that some players I played with during my time at Everton would have done better if the support was there with regards to coping with the pressure and the mental health side of things. When the boys are with us, they can see how close they are to the 'other side of the building' where the Under-23s and the first-team are, so there's definitely pressure on them.

ALL THE TEAMS ARE AT USM FINCH FARM TOGETHER, SO DOES DAVID UNSWORTH OCCASIONALLY COME OVER AND 'BORROW' SOME OF YOUR PLAYERS FOR AN UNDER-23 TRAINING SESSION, LEAVING YOU A BIT SHORT?

Yes, it happens all the time, but that's what we want. David's communication with us is very good and he lets us know as early as he possibly can when he needs any of our players, but obviously sometimes he'll get a late request from the first-team for some of his players. That's when we, as coaches, have to be adaptable. We need to have a Plan B, Plan C, etc, to make sure our training isn't affected and that the players left with us get a good quality session.

Sometimes I can dip into the Under-16s but, more often than not, they don't train at the same time as us because they are still schoolboys.

A boy can be playing really well for the Under-16s but then it's tough for him to play against 18-year-olds when he joins up with us. We assure them that we know there is a physical difference but it's good experience because they have to survive. It can help them develop because they have to read the game better and use their intuition and rely more on their technical and tactical ability rather than strength and power.

Anthony is certainly one of them. Like a lot of young players, his rise to the first-team hasn't been smooth – there have been a few dips along the way and the pathway for the boys can be what we call 'a bumpy road' but that's what drives the best ones on.

We want our young players to make it through to the first-team, that's why we're all here as coaches, but we need to protect them and make sure they don't get carried away with all the hype because a young player can quickly take his eye off the ball when he thinks he's cracked it. Some can think they no longer need to put the extra work in but that's definitely not the case with Anthony.

WHAT WAS IT LIKE HAVING TIM CAHILL HELPING OUT WITH YOUR COACHING SESSIONS LAST SEASON?

It was great! He was so enthusiastic, and he would have stayed out on the field with the lads all day if we'd allowed him to! I remember asking him one day to take a few of our strikers and midfielders to do a session on arriving in the penalty area to meet the ball - just what Tim was brilliant at when he played. I had to virtually drag him off the pitch in the end because the players were shattered! Tim absolutely loved it and we loved having him around.

HOW PROUD HAVE YOU BEEN OF ANTHONY GORDON, WHO HAS REALLY TAKEN HIS CHANCE WITH THE FIRST-TEAM?

I have been so impressed with the way he has conducted himself on and off the pitch. We like to produce well-rounded young men who know what it takes to be a professional footballer, and

WHO'S THE BOSS ...?

Here are TEN managers from the Premier League last season ...
but the photographs were taken during their playing days!

See how many you can name ...

ANSWERS

1 _____

2 _____

3 _____

4 _____

5 _____

6 _____

7 _____

8 _____

9 _____

10 _____

ASK A GROWN-UP ...!!

You may need some help with this photo quiz!

Here are some famous Premier League managers ... when they were a lot younger!
Between them they have won Premier Leagues, Champions Leagues, FA Cups,
League Cups and some have managed international teams!

How many of them can you recognise?

ANSWERS

1 _____

2 _____

3 _____

4 _____

5 _____

6 _____

7 _____

8 _____

9 _____

10 _____

Answers on pages 62-63

FAREWELL...
LEIGHTON BAINES

The last game of last season was the final appearance in the wonderful career of Leighton Baines.

The Everton left-back came off the bench against Bournemouth for his 420th, and last, match for the club.

Baines was signed from Wigan Athletic in the summer of 2007, but he wasn't an instant first-choice in his preferred position, owing to the excellent form of Joleon Lescott.

But when Lescott was moved to central defence, Baines got in...and stayed in!

Surprisingly, for someone with such a magnificent left foot, it took him 57 games before his first goal against Portsmouth at Fratton Park in March 2009.

He would go on to score 39 times for the Blues.

Later that season, Baines was one of the penalty takers in the FA Cup semi-final shoot-out at Wembley against Manchester United. Tim Cahill had missed Everton's first kick but Baines stepped forward to take the second and slammed the ball into the net.

The Blues eventually won 4-2 on penalties but lost in the final against Chelsea.

In the 2010/11 season, Baines played every minute of every Everton game and swept the board at the End of Season Awards event, winning the Player of the Year, Players' Player of the Year and Goal of the Season.

The goal that won it for him was a direct free-kick in the last minute of extra-time in an FA Cup replay against Chelsea. It earned Everton a 1-1 draw and the tie was won on penalties – although on this occasion Baines missed his kick!

However, as it wouldn't have even gone to penalties without his wonder-goal, he was quickly forgiven!

BAINES IS THE MOST SUCCESSFUL EVERTON PENALTY-TAKER OF ALL TIME – SCORING 25 OF THE 28 HE TOOK

He would win the Player of the Year again in 2013 and was voted Players' Player of the Year twice more, in 2011 and 2013.

Baines won 30 caps for England during his career after making his debut against Egypt at Wembley in March 2010. John Terry, Frank Lampard and Wayne Rooney were all in the England

Celebrating the 2009 FA Cup semi-final win with Tim Howard

team that night, as was Baines' future Everton team-mate Theo Walcott.

His one international goal came in September 2012 in a 5-0 win away to Moldova and he played in the 2014 World Cup finals in Brazil.

Other Everton highlights include two superb free-kicks in the same game against West Ham United in September 2013. They helped Everton win 3-2 at Upton Park in a game that saw Romelu Lukaku score the winner on his debut.

And supporters still talk about a free-kick that he scored at Newcastle United in January 2013. Baines was at least 30-yards out, but the ball travelled like a rocket and zoomed into the back of the net.

THANKS FOR THE MEMORIES LEIGHTON BAINES - YOU'RE AN

EVERTON LEGEND!

SIT DOWN...
WITH LUCAS DIGNE

WHAT IS YOUR FAVOURITE EVERTON GOAL?

Probably the first one I scored at Goodison Park against Watford a couple of years ago. It was a good goal and a perfect moment. It was very late in the game and it earned us a point because we were losing 2-1.

WHO WAS YOUR FAVOURITE PLAYER WHEN YOU WERE GROWING UP?

I want to give you two answers to this! I loved watching Zinedine Zidane and Thierry Henry. Zidane won the World Cup with France and he was just a great player with an amazing first touch. They were both world class players.

WHO IS THE BEST DANCER AT THE CLUB?

It would be between Moise Kean and Yerry Mina! They are both very good and so the level of competition between them would be very high!

WHAT IS YOUR FAVOURITE 'SCOUSE' PHRASE?

'Come on lad!'

WHO HAS BEEN YOUR TOUGHEST OPPONENT?

Easy one this... Lionel Messi. I played for Roma

against him in the Champions League and he was just amazing. You have to stay focussed for every second of the game because he is so quick and he thinks very quickly too.

WHAT'S BEEN THE BEST ATMOSPHERE THAT YOU'VE EVER PLAYED IN?

The Merseyside derby at Goodison against Liverpool in March 2019. The atmosphere was unbelievable.

BEST ATMOSPHERE!

WHO IS THE BEST SINGER IN THE SQUAD?

Well he's not the best but the one I like to listen to is Richarlison because he is so funny when he sings!

WHO IS YOUR BEST FRIEND AT EVERTON?

I get on well with everybody. The players at Everton are like one big family and that's one of the things I love about the club. We all get on very well together.

WHEN YOU WERE AT BARCELONA, DID YOU STUDY LIONEL MESSI TAKING FREE-KICKS?

We never practiced free-kicks at Barcelona! But everyone can learn from watching Lionel Messi.

WHAT TYPE OF MUSIC DO YOU LIKE?

I listen to a lot of Spanish music. My little son likes it too!

WHAT DO YOU THINK WHEN THE EVERTONIANS SING YOUR NAME?

It's amazing! When I heard it for the first time it was a fantastic moment for me and I would like to thank our fans. It makes me very proud.

WHAT IS YOUR FAVOURITE MOVIE?

'Man On Fire' with Denzil Washington. It's a great film and he is a brilliant actor.

WHAT NETFLIX SERIES DO YOU WATCH?

I like 'Power' about a nightclub owner. I have watched all the episodes and I enjoyed them. I also like watching the Formula 1 documentaries.

WHO HAS BEEN THE BIGGEST INSPIRATION IN YOUR CAREER?

My father, my mother and my brother because they have given me a lot of help and advice during my life. My father showed me how to be a good man.

YOU HAVE A LOT OF TATTOOS... WHICH IS YOUR FAVOURITE ONE?

Ha ha! I love all my tattoos, but I had a toy teddy bear and a toy rabbit done for my wife and my baby, so I'll pick that one.

NAME THE REF...

HOW WELL DO YOU KNOW THE MEN IN THE MIDDLE?

Here are ten Premier League referees and you've probably shouted at them at some point after they made a decision you didn't agree with!

BUT DO YOU RECOGNISE THEM?

See how many you get right ... and if it's **less than six**, give yourself a yellow card!
Less than four and it's a straight red!!

WHO'LL BE THE
WINNERS?!

As you're making your way through this year's fab Everton Annual, the 2020/21 season will already be starting to take shape... but who'll be lifting silverware at the end of it?

Here is a list of last season's winners - all you have to do is predict who will take the honours this year...

COMPETITION	2019/20 WINNERS	2020/21 WINNERS
PREMIER LEAGUE	LIVERPOOL	
CHAMPIONSHIP	LEEDS UNITED	
PROMOTED FROM THE CHAMPIONSHIP	WEST BROM AND FULHAM	
LEAGUE ONE	COVENTRY CITY	
LEAGUE TWO	SWINDON TOWN	
NATIONAL LEAGUE	BARROW	
FA CUP	ARSENAL	
LEAGUE CUP	MANCHESTER CITY	
WOMEN'S SUPER LEAGUE	CHELSEA	
SCOTTISH PREMIER LEAGUE	CELTIC	
UEFA CHAMPIONS LEAGUE	BAYERN MUNICH	
EUROPA LEAGUE	SEVILLA	
FOOTBALLER OF THE YEAR	JORDAN HENDERSON	
WHERE WILL EVERTON FINISH IN THE PREMIER LEAGUE?	12th	
WHO WILL BE EVERTON'S TOP GOLSCORER?	DOMINIC CALVERT-LEWIN & RICHARLSION (15 EACH)	
TOTAL		/15

EVERTON IN THE COMMUNITY

Max and Chris

During the global Covid-19 pandemic, Everton Football Club and Everton in the Community staff provided vital support and assistance to thousands of individuals and families in need across the city of Liverpool through our Blue Family initiative.

Delivered collaboratively by the club and our official charity, Blue Family helped to maintain contact with fans, former players and programme participants, as well as providing support to some of the most vulnerable and at-risk members of the community.

Thousands of check-in phone calls were made by staff, players from the first-team, Under-23 and Everton Women and Club Ambassadors. For example, Mason Holgate made telephone calls to fans, so did Richarlison and Carlo Ancelotti. Ambassadors Graeme Sharp, Ian Snodin and Graham Stuart made phone calls every single day for about four months to supporters who were either unwell, isolating or just feeling a bit

down because they couldn't celebrate special occasions in the manner they would have liked. David Unsworth got involved too, describing making the calls as 'truly humbling and one of the best things I've ever been involved in' and dozens of former players were contacted regularly to remind them the football club was there to help if we were needed.

Everton in the Community staff delivered more than a thousand emergency food parcels and distributed emergency foodbank vouchers to individuals and families living across Liverpool, in addition to purchasing and delivering medical prescriptions for the elderly and medicines for a terminally ill child.

In addition to buying emergency food and hygiene parcels and medical prescriptions, money

raised through Blue Family donations was also used to purchase gas and electricity vouchers, as well as to support other initiatives and charities across the city, including foodbanks.

The campaign also helped to fund food vouchers for local children living in poverty who lost access to free school meals, and households without essential kitchen equipment. It also allowed for the provision of meals for the homeless, housing support and help with funding for items such as TVs and radios for people who were self-isolating alone.

And millions of Blues all around the world tuned into our social media sites to watch exercise and mental health sessions, cookery demonstrations and bedtime stories, as well as accessing home-learning educational resources that had been compiled by first-team players and training staff across the Club and Everton in the Community. Everton in the Community's Neighbourhood team continues to be on hand to support the 10,000+ residents living within the immediate vicinity of Goodison Park – one of the most socially deprived areas in England – and has provided housing and money management support, as well as advice on benefits and Universal Credit. There has also been support for local refugees and asylum seekers through the charity's ongoing relationship with British Red Cross.
The last 18 months have also seen Everton in the Community's Youth Engagement team support 1,500 young people who are at risk of social isolation, domestic violence and criminal exploitation.

The club's training ground, USM Finch Farm, donated produce each week during April to the Blue Family campaign, which was delivered directly to North Liverpool foodbanks and was used to build emergency food parcels for local families in need.

Over Easter, Community Shop donated 500 Easter eggs to Blue Family, which Everton in the Community staff personally delivered to

participants from its Premier League Kicks programme, using the opportunity to engage with families and check-in with them during the difficult time. Eggs were also donated to Huyton Hey Manor Care Home to help lift residents' spirits, and to those living in the Blue Mile. Thanks to support from Alpha Taxis and Home Bargains, we were also able to deliver food and hygiene bags full of essential items, including nappies, baby wipes and baby milk to vulnerable, isolated and homeless individuals, as well as elderly residents and new mums living in the Blue Mile.

Meanwhile, a generous donation of £1,000 from Access Point UK was used to purchase microwave ovens for local families living in poverty who lacked basic cooking equipment and, prior to receiving a microwave through the Blue Family campaign, their child's only hot meal each day often came from their free school meal entitlement.

Additionally, residents living across Liverpool 4 saw their streets given an injection of colour when Aintree Racecourse kindly donated 40 hanging baskets to the Club's official charity. The bright and colourful hanging baskets were originally intended for use during The Randox Health Grand National 2020.

The Everton YouTube channel also staged a marathon on-line pop concert featuring local bands that raised thousands of pounds for the Blue Family campaign.

It was a worrying and difficult time for everybody but, as usual, Everton Football Club was there to help.

ABDOULAYE DACOURE

I was born on New Year's Day in 1993 in the town of Meulan-en-Yvelines in France.

I am the eldest of three brothers.

I started my professional career with Rennes, playing initially for the B team.

I made my debut in Ligue 1 during the 2012/13 season and scored against Stade Brest. It was a shot with my left foot!

Playing for Rennes against Paris St Germain

In 2016 I signed for Watford.

I was loaned out straight away to La Liga side, Granada.

I made my La Liga debut as a substitute again Real Madrid - my Everton team-mate James Rodriguez was in the Madrid team!

I played 15 times for Granada and helped the team to avoid relegation.

My last game for them was against Barcelona when I was against Andres Iniesta.

My Watford debut was in August 2016 against Chelsea at Vicarage Road. I replaced Etienne Capoue late in the game.

I scored my first Watford goal in March 2017, but we lost 4-3 against Southampton and my goal was a stoppage time consolation.

Celebrating a goal for Watford

I was voted the Watford Player of the Season at the end of the 2017/18 season ... and also the Players' Player of the Season

I played for Watford in the 2019 FA Cup final at Wembley, but we lost the game 6-0 to Manchester City.

I made 129 Premier League appearances for the Hornets, scoring 17 goals.

I have represented France at Under-17, 18, 19, 20 and 21 level. Paul Pogba and Raphael Varane were among my team-mates in the international youth teams.

In September 2020 I signed for Everton!

JARRAD BRANTHWAITE

WOW, WHAT A STORY!

Teenage centre-half Jarrad Branthwaite started the season playing for Carlisle United in League Two... and ended it playing in the Premier League for Everton and Carlo Ancelotti.

He made his professional debut in February 2019 at the age of 17 against Forest Green Rovers and less than twelve months later he was leaving Carlisle for Everton!

He made his Blues debut against Wolverhampton Wanderers in July 2020 and ended the season with four first-team appearances under his belt.

WHAT WAS IT LIKE FOR YOU TO PLAY IN THE FIRST-TEAM JARRAD?

It's been a whirlwind for me! To be playing first-team football in the Premier League at 18 is every boy's dream and I would never have believed it three months earlier, but I know I've got to keep working hard to push on.

Jarrad in action on his Everton debut against Wolves

You see players like Anthony Gordon getting a chance and doing well and it inspires young players to want to achieve the same thing. It pushes you to train even harder to try and get in and around the team. I've played in the first-team but the hard work is only just beginning for me really.

WHEN DID YOU FIND OUT THAT YOU WERE GOING TO ACTUALLY START YOUR FIRST GAME AGAINST ASTON VILLA AT GOODISON PARK?

I found out a couple of days before the game when we were doing team shape in training. I just had to keep my head down and get myself ready for it! I sent my parents a text as soon as I could and they were buzzing for me! There were a few nerves on the night before the game but on actual match-day I felt fine.

IS IT TRUE THAT THERE ARE A FEW BLUES IN THE BRANTHWAITE FAMILY?

Some of my uncles are Evertonians but some of the family are from Manchester and support Man City. My granddad is a massive City fan and although he wants me to do well, I won't be able to change him to Everton!

WHAT DOES CARLO ANCELOTTI SAY TO YOU?

Just to keep working as hard as I can. I know that I have loads of areas that I can still improve on to become a better player and that's what I am focussing on. The manager wants everyone to develop as a player so we can develop as a team. I still can't believe that I am learning from one of the best managers in the world. He's won so much and worked with so many world-class players and it's unbelievable for a young boy like me to be learning from him.

WHAT'S THE BIGGEST DIFFERENCE BETWEEN PLAYING FOR CARLISLE UNITED IN LEAGUE TWO AND EVERTON IN THE PREMIER LEAGUE?

League Two is more physical, more long balls and things like that. The Premier League is a lot faster and you have to be quicker on your feet. The pace of the games is the biggest thing I have had to adapt to. It's a hundred miles an hour with excellent quality on the ball and so I know I need to develop my game.

DUNCAN FERGUSON WAS A GREAT CENTRE-FORWARD WHO USED TO FRIGHTEN CENTRE-HALVES! HAS HE GIVEN YOU ANY TIPS?

Yes, I do one-v-one sessions with him in training. He was a great player and so that's helping me a lot. I can tell you that he's still the same as he was when he was playing! He's still got it!

PLAYING FIRST-TEAM FOOTBALL IN THE PREMIER LEAGUE AT 18 IS EVERY BOY'S DREAM

1

ANSWER

2

ANSWER

3

ANSWER

4

ANSWER

GROWN-UP

QUIZ

You'll probably need some help with this Picture Quiz!

Here are ten Everton players from the Premier League era - challenge a grown-up to name all ten inside **TWO MINUTES**!!

5

ANSWER

6

ANSWER

7

ANSWER

8

ANSWER

9

ANSWER

10

ANSWER

GYLFI SIGURDSSON

— SIT DOWN WITH —
MASON HOLGATE...

WHAT TYPE OF MUSIC DO YOU LIKE?

I know a lot of people say this but I pretty much like every type of music. Actually, I don't like house music when there are no words! I need lyrics in my music.

WHAT'S THE STRONGEST ASPECT OF YOUR GAME?

I like to bring the ball out from the back. I'm comfortable doing that.

WHAT DO YOU THINK YOU STILL NEED TO WORK ON?

I work on everything, including the strong parts of my game, because none of it is perfect and you have to keep striving to get better every day, especially at this level. You'll never get everything right every time but that's what you have to aim for.

DID YOUR LOAN SPELL AT WEST BROM HELP YOU AS A PLAYER?

Yes it did, definitely. It's probably the best thing I've ever done. Going there improved me because there was some consistency to my game with playing every week. You can't really replicate top-level match action in training.

ANY TIPS FOR A YOUNG PLAYER WHO HAS SWITCHED POSITION FROM CENTRE-HALF TO FULL-BACK?

You have to have confidence in yourself and don't go out onto the pitch thinking that you're playing out of position. If you're good enough to be in the team, you'll be fine and you just need to keep telling yourself 'this is my position'. Maybe play things nice and safe at first.

WHO'S THE FUNNIEST PLAYER IN THE DRESSING ROOM?

I would have to say Tom Davies because he's always up to something! If someone pulls a prank in the dressing room, Tom is the first person we all look at!

WHO'S YOUR FAVOURITE BETWEEN TOM DAVIES AND DOMINIC CALVERT-LEWIN?

What a question! You know what, I genuinely couldn't pick between them, they're both really close friends of mine. We're not just team-mates, we are great mates off the pitch as well.

WHAT'S YOUR FAVOURITE BISCUIT?

Easiest question of the lot! Chocolate fingers every time!

WHAT WAS IT LIKE SCORING YOUR FIRST GOAL FOR EVERTON AGAINST WATFORD IN THE LEAGUE CUP?

It was brilliant! The lads were having a joke with me because I still hadn't scored for Everton and to be fair, I'm not great at scoring goals in training! Jordan Pickford told me that I would never score so to finally get one was great. Have that Jordan!!

WHAT DID YOU THINK WHEN YOU HEARD THAT CARLO ANCELOTTI WAS GOING TO BE THE MANAGER?

All the lads were very excited about it. When you look at the teams he's managed, the players he's worked with and the trophies that he's won, it's unbelievable. I'm loving every moment of learning from him. If you can't learn from someone

like Carlo Ancelotti, then you shouldn't be playing football.

WHO'S THE BEST PLAYER YOU'VE EVER PLAYED AGAINST?

Eden Hazard when he was at Chelsea. He can go either way when he's running at you because he's a great player on both sides, so it was really difficult to mark him.

WOULD YOU LIKE TO BE THE EVERTON CAPTAIN ONE DAY?

Well, obviously, that would be a massive honour but Seamus is a fantastic captain and he's helped me so much ever since I've been at the club. If I can one day be as good a captain as he is, then I'll be very happy, because the whole dressing room has got so much respect for Seamus.

WHO'S THE BEST DANCER IN THE SQUAD?

Some dance more than others but that doesn't mean that they are the best. It depends what kind of music it is! Moise Kean and Alex Iwobi are always dancing and Dominic Calvert-Lewin is a good dancer. In fact, I'll give the 'Best Dancer' prize to Dom!

YOUR questions...

1 Favourite Everton player?

2 Best Everton game you've ever seen?

3 Favourite TV programme?

4 Best film you've ever seen?

JAMES RODRIGUEZ

His full name is James David Rodriguez Rubio.

He was born on 12 July 1991 in the city of Cucuta, in the north east of Colombia.

He started his career with Colombian 2nd Division side Envigado and made his professional debut at the age of just 14!

When he was 17, James moved to Argentina and signed for Club Atletico Banfield.

He won the Argentine Premier Division with Banfield in 2009.

His tremendous form soon attracted the interest of European clubs and in 2010 James moved to FC Porto.

With Porto, he won three Portuguese league titles, the Portuguese Cup and the Europa League.

In 2011, aged 20, James made his international debut for Colombia.

In May 2013 he signed for French side AS Monaco for a reported fee of 45m euros.

James was a star of the 2014 World Cup in Brazil. He was part of the Colombia team that reached the quarter-finals for the first time (they lost to the hosts) and he finished the tournament as the leading scorer with six goals.

After the World Cup he signed for Real Madrid, managed by Carlo Ancelotti.

During his time at the Bernabeu, James won two La Liga titles but didn't play in either of the Champions League finals that Madrid won while he was there.

In 2017 he signed a two-year loan deal with Bayern Munich, with whom he won the Bundesliga twice. His spell in Germany reunited him with Carlo Ancelotti.

He returned to Madrid for the 2019/20 season and joined Everton in September 2020.

IZZY CHRISTIANSEN

ENGLAND INTERNATIONAL IZZY CHRISTIANSEN JOINED EVERTON LAST SEASON FROM FRENCH TEAM OLYMPIQUE LYON ...

WHEN DID YOU START TO PLAY FOOTBALL?

Like a lot of female footballers, I started playing the game with my elder brother and his mates. I was always out in the countryside or on the local school pitch and would play until it got dark. I was also allowed in the club scout football team in the Macclesfield & District League, which was a good, competitive league. I played on the right wing.

It was just a pastime for me because at that time it wasn't possible for a young girl to dream about being a professional footballer. The girls can aspire to that now. They can be footballers. It's so important for young girls to have their own female football role models, like the England Women international players. When I was growing up, my role model was Frank Lampard.

HOW DID YOUR CAREER MOVE FORWARD?

I was actually at the Everton School of Excellence but there was no professional league in this country when I was 18-years-old, so my option was further education and I went to Birmingham University to do my degree. I played for Birmingham City FC, who were part-time, and then became a professional when I signed for Manchester City in 2014.

WHAT WAS IT LIKE AT MANCHESTER CITY?

When I first went there, City didn't have a team in WSL so they were starting from scratch but the squad was built up slowly and in time I won everything that it's possible to win domestically and played in the semi-final of the Champions League. I really enjoyed it there but when the opportunity came for me to play abroad, I took it.

YOU MUST HAVE BEEN VERY PROUD TO WIN THE WSL PLAYERS' PLAYER OF THE YEAR AWARD IN 2016?

Yes I was and I still can't believe that I won it. I wish I would have enjoyed the evening more, but it was all just a blur! I had no idea that I had won, although I had been told to wear something nice but I thought that was because I had been nominated. There were so many famous faces in the room when I got up to accept the award - Eden Hazard won the men's award.

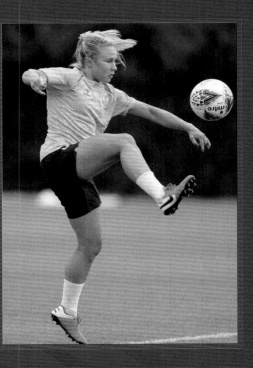

YOU LEFT CITY IN 2018 TO JOIN OLYMPIQUE LYON IN FRANCE ...

I wouldn't say it had been a dream or an ambition to play abroad but when the opportunity came along I wasn't going to let it pass. At the time, Lyon were arguably the best women's football team in the world and they probably still are.

I had been five years at Manchester City and we had a very structured way of playing and moving to France showed me that it doesn't always have to be that way. The football with Lyon was more free-spirited and the players could move about the pitch with more freedom. I loved it and we got crowds of 15-20,000 for our Champions League games.

AND THEN IT WAS BACK TO THE UK TO JOIN EVERTON!

I was very motivated after speaking to Willie Kirk prior to signing for Everton. I know what the Club is all about, having been at the Centre of Excellence when I was younger. I know about the rich history of Everton Women's football and it's so exciting to be a part of it. At the end of the day we want to win things and I would love to see us competing for a Champions League place. The squad is brilliant and the sky is the limit for Everton. We've got our new stadium at Walton Hall Park, which is obviously close to Goodison, and I hope we get loads of Evertonians coming out to support us.

IZZY'S FAVOURITE FIVE SONGS		YOUR FAVOURITE FIVE SONGS	
Beautiful South	Everybody's Talking		
Haim	Falling		
Mumford and Sons	Believe		
Tina Turner	Proud Mary		
Take That	Greatest Day		

A MERRY CHRISTMAS TO YOU ALL FROM EVERYONE AT EVERTON FOOTBALL CLUB!

How about designing your own Blues Christmas card?

Here's a blank one – you can have any design you like.

You can stick photos in, draw the players, have Santa in an Everton kit or even have pictures of yourself – anything you like!

It's your Christmas card – you choose the design!

TEENAGE SENSATIONS ...!

The Everton Academy has an excellent record of producing players for the first-team. Here are eleven who played for the Blues in the Premier League while they were still teenagers.

See how many of them you can name...

1 ANSWER

2 ANSWER

3 ANSWER

4 ANSWER

5 ANSWER

6 ANSWER

7 ANSWER

8 ANSWER

9 ANSWER

10 ANSWER

11 ANSWER

ANSWERS ON PAGES 62-63

47

CHARLIE

JACK

ARCHIE

ALFIE & SOPHIA

HARRISON

ALFIE & FRANKIE

ALL
TOGETHER
NOW

Ev
NIL SATIS

SIAN, CARYS & FFION

ISAAC

LILLIA

ARLO

JACK & HARVEY

SKYLER

OLIVER

STEPHEN

ESME

CHARLIE

ISLA

LUNA & ISLA

CHARLIE & MELODIE

HERE'S A SELECTION OF YOUNG BLUES PROUDLY WEARING THEIR COLOURS ...

JOSH

CHARLIE

JUDE

IT'S A GRAND OLD TEAM TO PLAY FOR AND IT'S A GRAND OLD TEAM TO SUPPORT AND IF YOU KNOW YOUR HISTORY IT'S ENOUGH TO MAKE YOUR HEART GO WOAH

JOSEPH

JACK, CHLOE & EVIE

LUKE

JOSH

OLIVER

49

JORDAN PICKFORD

WHO HAS GOT THE HARDEST SHOT IN TRAINING?
I have to say Gylfi. His power, placement and technique make his shots so hard to save.

WHAT'S YOUR FAVOURITE EVER SAVE?
The one in added time against Colombia in the World Cup in 2018. It was a rocket of a shot that was arrowing straight for the top left-hand corner and I wasn't expecting it because it was from 35-yards out, so I was quite pleased to turn it away. Just a shame that Yerry Mina then equalised from the corner! But we won on penalties!

WHO IS THE WORST DRESSER BETWEEN TOM DAVIES AND DOMINIC CALVERT-LEWIN?
They're both up there with the worst I've seen, but I'll go for Dom!

WHAT'S YOUR FAVOURITE BISCUIT?
Wow! There's plenty to choose from for me, I've got lots of favourites, but if I had to choose one it would be caramel digestives!

PICK YOUR FAVOURITE GAME IN AN EVERTON SHIRT ...
The 2-1 away win at Newcastle United last December. I was nice and solid and I dictated the game from my point of view. After losing at St James's Park the season before I needed to show some character and I did that.

Favourite game – Newcastle away

Favourite save – Colombia in the World Cup

Jordan and Mason Holgate

WHAT ADVICE WOULD YOU GIVE A 9-YEAR-OLD WHO PLAYS IN GOAL FOR HIS LOCAL TEAM?

Just enjoy it, because that's the main thing, having fun and learning as you go along. I played for my local teams from the age of 5 and I loved it. And enjoy making saves as well – it doesn't matter how you make them, just get in the way of the ball.

IF YOU WEREN'T A GOALKEEPER, WHAT POSITION WOULD YOU PLAY?

I would say centre-midfield. When I was a kid at school I always played in that position. I loved tackling and I loved trying to spray a few diagonal passes!

WHY DID YOU BECOME A GOALKEEPER?

When I was younger, I was a bit mad and my older brother was a centre-forward so he would line me up in the street outside the house and fire shots at me and I would dive all over the place trying to save them. I went to watch my brother once and there was a little team training nearby who didn't have a keeper so I went over and asked if I could play. It just went from there.

WHICH OUTFIELD PLAYER AT EVERTON WOULD BE THE BEST GOALKEEPER?

It's got to be Seamus Coleman! He played Gaelic Football when he was younger and sometimes after training he likes to go in goal and face a few shots.

DID YOU WATCH THE NETFLIX SERIES ABOUT YOUR OLD CLUB, SUNDERLAND?

I watched the first series, but I didn't enjoy it because it wasn't a good time for Sunderland. But it's a great series for showing the passion of the supporters. The Sunderland fans are very similar to the Evertonians in the way they love the club and always support the team.

WHAT GOES THROUGH YOUR MIND WHEN YOU'RE TRYING TO SAVE A PENALTY?

Well mentally, I always think I'm going to save every one. That doesn't happen, of course, but I do a lot of research on the penalty takers. You need a bit of luck as well, but that research can often help and I've saved a few in the past.

WHAT WAS THE FIRST RECORD YOU EVER BOUGHT?

It was a favourite song of both my mum and me. It's called 'I'll Fly With You' by Gigi D'Agostino and it's an absolute banger! I still listen to it now.

WHO'S YOUR BEST MATE AT THE CLUB?

Mason Holgate. When I first joined Everton I knew Mason from playing alongside him for England Under-21s and he taught me a lot about the club and we always have a good bit of banter between us.

LOVE EVERTON?
Of course you do!

LOVE SOCIAL MEDIA?
Of course you do!

Well, the two go hand-in-hand – here's your guide to all our social media content ...

Like us @everton for daily news, videos, interviews with the manager, his staff and all your favourite players. And you can watch loads of exclusive live events!

Follow us @everton and be the first to hear about breaking news such as new signings, team news and much more! Check out daily images from behind the scenes as well as interviews with the Everton stars.

Make sure you follow us on TikTok, @everton - our newest social media account! Launched at the start of 2020, we've joined in with a host of fun trends and shown our players in a completely different light.

Follow us at 'everton' for current and classic images from the club, as well as our stories including matchday and behind-the-scenes coverage. See the stuff that you can't see anywhere else!

 YouTube

Offering exclusive video content from Goodison Park and USM Finch Farm, including interviews and plenty of behind-the-scenes footage. You can also enjoy classic matches and moments from our illustrious history. Re-live the glory days of the 1980s for example!

Spotify

The Official Everton Podcast is available to stream on all your usual podcast providers. Offering a range of in-depth interviews, we speak to Everton legends about their time at the club and much, much more! Hear from Tim Howard, Landon Donovan, Richard Gough, Joleon Lescott, Gary Lineker and plenty more besides ...

Watch classic matches like the 1984 FA Cup final on YouTube

Catch DCL's latest fashion statement on Instagram!

See Carlo's interviews on our Facebook page

PLAYLISTS:

Your Everton stars have selected their mix-ups, and so has the boss Carlo Ancelotti ...

NAME THE PLAYER...

Here are 19 players who appeared in the Premier League last season. All you have to do is name the player and the team he was playing for...

1

PLAYER: ....

TEAM: ....

2

PLAYER: ....

TEAM: ....

3

PLAYER: ....

TEAM: ....

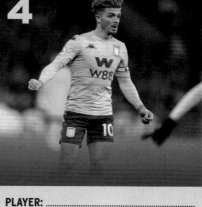

4

PLAYER: ....

TEAM: ....

5

PLAYER: ....

TEAM: ....

6

PLAYER: ....

TEAM: ....

7

PLAYER: ....

TEAM: ....

8

PLAYER: ....

TEAM: ....

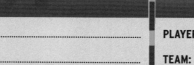

9

PLAYER: ....

TEAM: ....

10

PLAYER: ....

TEAM: ....

11

PLAYER: ....

TEAM: ....

12

PLAYER: ....

TEAM: ....

13

PLAYER: ....

TEAM: ....

14

PLAYER: ....

TEAM: ....

15

PLAYER: ....

TEAM: ....

16

PLAYER: ....

TEAM: ....

17

PLAYER: ....

TEAM: ....

18

PLAYER: ....

TEAM: ....

19

PLAYER: ....

TEAM: ....

ANSWERS ON PAGE 63

DOMINIC CALVERT-LEWIN

WORDSEARCH

Hidden inside this grid of jumbled up letters are the names of TWELVE famous football teams. See how quickly you can find them all...

```
N P S K D H T M T E N J
O L Y E T J L K Y L K F
T K R L V E Q E F T L M
P E F X E L L L M S A F
M V L D Y N O A P A N T
A E S F R C H W M C E R
H R L U U N Q K N W S A
T T B C E L T I C E R N
U O N T K Y H M V N A G
O N T W T N N A W T C E
S O M L T R Y M M L Q R
T L O O P R E V I L G S
```

ARSENAL	**LIVERPOOL**
BURNLEY	**NEWCASTLE**
CELTIC	**RANGERS**
EVERTON	**SOUTHAMPTON**
FULHAM	**TOTTENHAM**
LEEDS	**WOLVES**

DAVID UNSWORTH

Hi everyone – you all know me as the manager of the Everton Under-23 team.

Here are a few more facts about my career that perhaps you didn't know ...

I scored a goal on my professional debut for Everton when I was 18-years-old. It was against Tottenham Hotspur at White Hart Lane. We were 3-0 down with 25 minutes to go and we came back to draw 3-3! I scored the equaliser in the 82nd minute, ten minutes after coming on as a substitute!

I won the FA Cup with Everton in 1995 when we beat Manchester United in the final at Wembley.

In 1997, Harry Redknapp signed me for West Ham United.

A year later I joined Aston Villa but before I could play a game for them, Everton wanted to sign me again so I came back to Goodison Park!

I was known for being a good penalty taker during my playing career. For Everton, I took 26 spot-kicks and scored from 23 of them, which was a record until Leighton Baines took it from me!

When David Moyes took over as manager in 2002, I scored the first goal of his first game after just 28 seconds against Fulham!

My 302 Premier League appearances for the Blues has only been bettered by Tim Howard, Leon Osman, Leighton Baines and Phil Jagielka.

In all matches for Everton I played 350 times and scored 40 goals.

I played once for England - against Japan at Wembley in June 1995. Gary Neville, Paul Gascoigne and Alan Shearer were amongst my team-mates.

After leaving Everton in 2004, I played for Portsmouth, Ipswich Town, Sheffield United, Wigan Athletic, Burnley and Huddersfield Town.

Before returning to the Blues as the Under-23 manager, I coached at Preston North End and Sheffield United.

I have had two separate spells as the caretaker manager of the Everton first-team.

AFTER LEAVING EVERTON I HAD SPELLS AT PORTSMOUTH, SHEFFIELD UNITED AND WIGAN ATHLETIC

MEET MY 2020/21 UNDER-23 SQUAD ....

BOBBY **CARROLL**

CON **OUZOUNIDIS**

EINAR **IVERSEN**

JOE **ANDERSON**

KYLE **JOHN**

LEWIS **DOBBIN**

MACKENZIE **HUNT**

NICOLAS **DEFREITAS-HANSEN**

NIELS **NKOUNKOU**

RHYS **HUGHES**

RYAN **ASTLEY**

SEBASTIAN **QUIRK**

ELLIS **SIMMS**

TYLER **ONYANGO**

HARRY **TYRER**

JOAO **VIRGINIA**

ZAN-LUK **LEBAN**

YOU ARE THE BOSS!

WHO DO YOU THINK ARE THE BEST PLAYERS IN THE WORLD?

WHO WOULD BE IN YOUR CURRENT WORLD XI?

WE ASKED OUR TEENAGE STRIKER ANTHONY GORDON TO PICK HIS - WHAT DO YOU THINK OF IT?

CAN YOU PICK A BETTER TEAM?

HAVE A GO ... AND SEE WHO MAKES YOUR STARTING ELEVEN ...

GORDON'S WORLD TEAM

"Well if I am the manager, then I'll have Pep Guardiola as my assistant, and we will be playing a 4-3-3 formation ..."

Kevin De Bruyne

Alphonso Davies

Kylian Mbappe

Lionel Messi

Neymar

Sergio Ramos

Goalkeeper:	MARC-ANDRE TER STEGEN (Barcelona)
Right-Back:	TRENT ALEXANDER-ARNOLD (Liverpool ... sorry)
Centre-Back:	SERGIO RAMOS (Real Madrid)
Centre-Back:	RAPHAEL VARANE (Real Madrid)
Left-Back:	ALPHONSO DAVIES (Bayern Munich)
Midfield:	TONY KROOS (Real Madrid)
Midfield:	KEVIN DE BRUYNE (Manchester City)
Midfield:	LIONEL MESSI (Barcelona)
Right-Wing:	KYLIAN MBAPPE (Paris St Germain)
Centre-Forward:	ROBERT LEWANDOWSKI (Bayern Munich)
Left-Wing:	NEYMAR (Paris St Germain)

WOULD YOU HAVE CHRISTIANO RONALDO IN THERE?
OR ANTOINE GRIEZMANN? OR MAYBE DAVID SILVA?

WHAT ABOUT KARIM BENZEMA, LUIS SUAREZ, JADON SANCHO,
LUKA MODRIC OR ERLING BRAUT HAALAND?

AND WHAT ABOUT YOUR ASSISTANT MANAGER?
PERHAPS CARLO ANCELOTTI!

MAYBE JOSE MOURINHO, ZINEDINE ZIDANE OR DIEGO SIMEONE?

MANAGER (Your name)	
ASSISTANT MANAGER	
FORMATION	

POSITION	PLAYER	CLUB

QUIZ ANSWERS

PAGE 17 - SEAMUS COLEMAN ANSWERS

1 David Moyes
2 Blackpool
3 Stephen Kenny
4 Phil Jagielka
5 Gaelic Football

PAGE 18-19

1 **Andre Gomes** - Benfica
2 **Seamus Coleman** - Blackpool
3 **Michael Keane** - Leicester City
4 **Dominic Calvert-Lewin** - Northampton
5 **Alex Iwobi** - Arsenal
6 **Lucas Digne** - Paris St Germain
7 **Yerry Mina** - Barcelona
8 **Theo Walcott** - Southampton
9 **Fabian Delph** - Leeds United
10 **Mason Holgate** - Barnsley
11 **Gylfi Sigurdsson** - Reading
12 **Jordan Pickford** - Preston North End

PAGE 21

Answer -
Dominic Calvert-Lewin

PAGE 24

1 Roy Hodgson
2 Frank Lampard
3 Nigel Pearson
4 Chris Wilder
5 Pep Guardiola
6 David Moyes
7 Mikel Arteta
8 Dean Smith
9 Steve Bruce
10 Graham Potter

PAGE 25

1 Terry Venables
2 Sir Alex Ferguson
3 Ron Atkinson
4 Walter Smith
5 George Graham
6 Graham Taylor
7 Bobby Robson
8 Brian Clough
9 Harry Redknapp
10 Sam Allardyce